Preface

From the Paris Commune of 1871, to the Russian and Cuban revolutions and other struggles for national liberation and socialism in this century, the propertied classes have always laid the charge of "terrorism" on the young fighters leading the struggle against exploitation and oppression. But it has been the terror of the capitalist rulers—whether through fascist tyranny or the use of their police forces and armies under bourgeois democracy—against which an outraged majority eventually rises.

Drawing on lessons from the revolutionary struggle in tsarist Russia, Leon Trotsky explains why the working class is the only social force capable of leading the toiling majority in overthrowing the capitalist exploiters and beginning the construction of a new society. Individual terrorism, whatever its intention, more and more relegates the makers of history to the role of spectators and opens the workers movement to provocation and victimization. In the four selections in this pamphlet, Trotsky explains the conclusions Marxists have drawn since the dawn of the modern communist movement. In the process he answers those who slander the revolutionary working-class movement as "terrorists" and "adventurists."

Leon Trotsky was a central leader of the October 1917 revolution in Russia. During the early years of the Soviet Republic he served at Lenin's request as foreign minister and head of the Red Army, and was a founding leader of the Communist International. Following the death of V.I. Lenin in 1924, Trotsky fought to continue Lenin's communist course in the face of the political counterrevolution that threw up Joseph Stalin as its chief representative. Expelled from the Soviet Union in 1929, Trotsky continued to lead revolutionary workers around the world to rebuild an international communist movement. He was assassinated in Mexico by Stalin's secret police in 1940.

The first two selections—"On Terrorism" and "The Collapse of Terror and Its Party"—were written following the Russian revolution of 1905. In these articles, Trotsky polemicizes against the strategic orientations of revolutionary organizations such as Narodnaya Volya (People's Will) and the Social Revolutionary Party, which advocated and organized individual acts of terror against hated tsarist officials.

In "Terrorism and the Stalinist Regime in the Soviet Union," from 1937, Trotsky explains why revolutionary workers opposed to the systematic terror of Stalin's regime would not respond in kind. Trotsky wrote the final selection, "For Grynszpan: Against the Fascist Pogrom Gangs and Stalinist Scoundrels," in response to the assassination in 1938 of a Nazi official at the German embassy in Paris by Herschel Grynszpan. While offering his "open moral solidarity" to this politically inexperienced young Jew, and condemning Grynszpan's "democratic" jailers, Trotsky makes a case as compelling today as it was in 1938, as he urges youth who might consider emulating Grynszpan's self-sacrificing example to seek the road of building a revolutionary workers party.

In these articles, the Russian Bolshevik leader reaffirms the Marxist strategy based on the efforts of the working class to advance the interests of the exploited majority and defend them and their organizations against the brutal oppression of the landlords and capitalists. In his 1920 book *Terrorism and Communism*, Trotsky defends the use of revolutionary violence by workers and peasants against the tsarist White Guards and imperialist armies invading the Soviet Republic. He exposes the permanent violence and brutality against the toilers inextricably rooted in the capitalist democracy and bourgeois pacifism defended by Karl Kautsky, a prominent leader of the Socialist International. Kautsky claimed the Bolsheviks had forsaken Marxism in favor of adventurism, despotism, and terror. Lenin also refuted Kautsky's charges and defended the course of the Bolshevik leadership in

The Proletarian Revolution and the Renegade Kautsky.

In this second edition of this pamphlet, first published in 1974, Pathfinder has restored the titles that appeared on Trotsky's articles when they were originally published in the opening four decades of this century. The entire text has been scanned and reset.

Jack Barnes
July 2, 1995

On terrorism

This article originally appeared in the November 1911 issue of *Der Kampf,* the theoretical monthly of the Austrian Social Democracy. Trotsky wrote it at the request of Friedrich Adler, the editor of *Der Kampf.*

Our class enemies are in the habit of complaining about our terrorism. What they mean by this is rather unclear. They would like to label all the activities of the proletariat directed against the class enemy's interests as terrorism. The strike, in their eyes, is the principal method of terrorism. The threat of a strike, the organization of strike pickets, an economic boycott of a slave-driving boss, a moral boycott of a traitor from our own ranks—all this and much more they call terrorism. If terrorism is understood in this way as any action inspiring fear in, or doing harm to, the enemy, then of course the entire class struggle is nothing but terrorism. And the only question remaining is whether the bourgeois politicians have the right to pour out their floods of moral indignation about proletarian terrorism when their entire state apparatus with its laws, police, and army is nothing but an apparatus for capitalist terror!

However, it must be said that when they reproach us with terrorism, they are trying—although not always consciously—

to give this word a narrower, less indirect meaning. The damaging of machines by workers, for example, is terrorism in this strict sense of the word. The killing of an employer, a threat to set fire to a factory or a death threat to its owner, an assassination attempt, with revolver in hand, against a government minister—all these are terrorist acts in the full and authentic sense. However, anyone who has an idea of the true nature of international Social Democracy ought to know that it has always opposed this kind of terrorism, and done so in the most irreconcilable way.

Why?

"Terrorizing" with the threat of a strike, or actually conducting a strike, is something only industrial or agricultural workers can do. The social significance of a strike depends directly upon first, the size of the enterprise or the branch of industry that it affects; and second, the degree to which the workers taking part in it are organized, disciplined, and ready for action. This is just as true of a political strike as it is of an economic one. It continues to be the method of struggle that flows directly from the productive role of the proletariat in modern society.

In order to develop, the capitalist system needs a parliamentary superstructure. But because it cannot confine the modern proletariat to a political ghetto, it must sooner or later allow the workers to participate in parliament. In elections, the mass character of the proletariat and its level of political development—qualities which, again, are determined by its social role, i.e., above all, its productive role—find their expression.

As in a strike, in elections the method, aim, and result of the struggle always depend on the social role and strength of the proletariat as a class.

Only the workers can conduct a strike. Artisans ruined by the factory, peasants whose water the factory is poisoning, or lumpen proletarians, in search of plunder, can smash machines, set fire to a factory, or murder its owner.

Only the conscious and organized working class can send a strong representation into the halls of parliament to look out for proletarian interests. However, in order to murder a prominent official you need not have the organized masses behind you. The recipe for explosives is accessible to all, and a Browning can be obtained anywhere.

In the first case, there is a social struggle, whose methods and means flow necessarily from the nature of the prevailing social order; in the second, a purely mechanical reaction identical everywhere—in China as in France—very striking in its outward form (murder, explosions, and so forth) but absolutely harmless as far as the social system goes.

A strike, even of modest size, has social consequences: strengthening of the workers' self-confidence, growth of the trade union, and not infrequently, even an improvement in production technology. The murder of a factory owner produces effects of a police nature only, or a change of proprietors devoid of any social significance.

Whether a terrorist attempt, even a "successful" one, throws the ruling class into confusion depends on the concrete political circumstances. In any case the confusion can only be short-lived; the capitalist state does not base itself on government ministers and cannot be eliminated with them. The classes it serves will always find new people; the mechanism remains intact and continues to function.

But the disarray introduced into the ranks of the working masses themselves by a terrorist attempt is much deeper. If it is enough to arm oneself with a pistol in order to achieve one's goal, why the efforts of the class struggle? If a thimbleful of gunpowder and a little chunk of lead is enough to shoot the enemy through the neck, what need is there for a class organization? If it makes sense to terrify highly placed personages with the roar of explosions, where is the need for a party? Why meetings, mass agitation, and elections if one can so easily take aim at the ministerial bench from the gallery of parliament?

In our eyes, individual terror is inadmissible precisely because it *belittles the role of the masses in their own consciousness,* reconciles them to their powerlessness, and turns their eyes and hopes toward a great avenger and liberator who some day will come and accomplish his mission.

The anarchist prophets of "the propaganda of the deed" can argue all they want about the elevating and stimulating influence of terrorist acts on the masses. Theoretical considerations and political experience prove otherwise. The more "effective" the terrorist acts, the greater their impact, the more the attention of the masses is focused on them—the more they reduce the interest of the masses in self-organization and self-education.

But the smoke from the explosion clears away, the panic disappears, the successor of the murdered minister makes his appearance, life again settles into the old rut, the wheel of capitalist exploitation turns as before; only police repression grows more savage and brazen. And as a result, in place of the kindled hopes and artificially aroused excitement come disillusion and apathy.

The efforts of reaction to put an end to strikes and to the mass workers movement in general have always, everywhere, ended in failure. Capitalist society needs an active, mobile, and intelligent proletariat; it cannot, therefore, bind the proletariat hand and foot for very long. On the other hand the anarchist "propaganda of the deed" has shown every time that the state is much richer in the means of physical destruction and mechanical repression than are the terrorist groups.

If that is so, where does it leave the revolution? Is it negated or rendered impossible by this state of affairs? Not at all. For the revolution is not a simple aggregate of mechanical means. The revolution can arise only out of the sharpening of the class struggle, and it can find a guarantee of victory only in the social functions of the proletariat. The mass political strike, the armed insurrection, the conquest of state power—all this is determined by the degree to which production has been developed, the alignment of class forces, the proletariat's social weight, and finally, by the social composition of the army, since the armed forces are the factor that in time of revolution determines the fate of state power.

Social Democracy is realistic enough not to try to avoid the revolution that is developing out of the existing historical conditions; on the contrary, it is moving to meet the revolution with eyes wide open. But—contrary to the anarchists and in direct struggle against them—Social Democracy rejects all methods and means that have as their goal to artificially force the development of society and to substitute chemical preparations for the insufficient revolutionary strength of the proletariat.

Before it is elevated to the level of a method of political struggle, terrorism makes its appearance in the form of individual acts of revenge. So it was in Russia, the classic land of terrorism. The flogging of political prisoners impelled Vera Zasulich to give expression to the general feeling of indignation by an assassination attempt on General Trepov. Her example was imitated in the circles of the revolutionary intelligentsia, who lacked any mass support. What began as an act of unthinking revenge was developed into an entire system in 1879–81.* The outbreaks of anarchist assassination attempts in Western Europe and North America always come after some atrocity committed by the government—the shooting of strikers or executions of political opponents. The most important psychological source of terrorism is always the feeling of revenge in search of an outlet.

There is no need to belabor the point that Social Democracy has nothing in common with those bought-and-paid-for moralists who, in response to any terrorist act, make solemn declarations about the "absolute value" of human life. These are the same people who, on other occasions, in the name of other absolute values—for example, the nation's honor or the monarch's prestige—are ready to shove millions of people into the hell of war. Today their national hero is the minister who gives the orders

---

* A reference to the People's Will terrorist organization, which succeeded in killing Tsar Alexander II in 1881.

for unarmed workers to be fired on—in the name of the most sacred right of private property; and tomorrow, when the desperate hand of the unemployed worker is clenched into a fist or picks up a weapon, they will start in with all sorts of nonsense about the inadmissibility of violence in any form.

Whatever the eunuchs and pharisees of morality may say, the feeling of revenge has its rights. It does the working class the greatest moral credit that it does not look with vacant indifference upon what is going on in this best of all possible worlds. Not to extinguish the proletariat's unfulfilled feeling of revenge, but on the contrary to stir it up again and again, to deepen it, and to direct it against the real causes of all injustice and human baseness—that is the task of Social Democracy.

If we oppose terrorist acts, it is only because *individual* revenge does not satisfy us. The account we have to settle with the capitalist system is too great to be presented to some functionary called a minister. To learn to see all the crimes against humanity, all the indignities to which the human body and spirit are subjected, as the twisted outgrowths and expressions of the existing social system, in order to direct all our energies into a collective struggle against this system—that is the direction in which the burning desire for revenge can find its highest moral satisfaction.

The collapse of terror
and its party

This is an excerpt from an article that originally appeared in the Russian socialist newspaper *Pravda*, March 27, 1909.

The article was written as an analysis of the sensational exposures concerning Yevno Azef, a top leader of the terrorist Combat Organization of the Social Revolutionary Party. In early 1909 Azef was exposed as an agent of the tsarist secret police. In the course of his work as an agent provocateur, Azef was even successful in organizing the assassination of the minister of the department that employed him.

The remaining two-thirds of this article can be found in the February 1, 1974, issue of the *Militant,* a weekly socialist newspaper, which published the article in its entirety.

For a whole month, the attention of everyone who was able to read and reflect at all, both in Russia and throughout the world, has been focused on Azef. His "case" is known to one and all from the legal newspapers and from accounts of the Duma debates over the demand raised by Duma deputies for an interpellation about Azef.

Now Azef has had time to recede into the background. His

name appears less and less frequently in the newspapers. However, before once and for all heaving Azef to the garbage heap of history, we think it necessary to sum up the main political lessons—not as regards the machinations of the Azef types *per se,* but with regard to terrorism as a whole, and to the attitude toward it held by the main political parties in the country.

Individual terror as a method for political revolution is our Russian "national" contribution.

Of course, the killing of "tyrants" is almost as old as the institution of "tyranny" itself; and poets of all centuries have composed more than a few hymns in honor of the liberating dagger.

But systematic terror, taking as its task the elimination of satrap after satrap, minister after minister, monarch after monarch—"Sashka after Sashka,"* as an 1880s Narodnaya Volya [People's Will] member familiarly formulated the program for terror—this kind of terror, adjusting itself to absolutism's bureaucratic hierarchy and creating its own revolutionary bureaucracy, is the product of the unique creative powers of the Russian intelligentsia.

Of course, there must be deep-seated reasons for this—and we should seek them, first, in the nature of the Russian autocracy and, second, in the nature of the Russian intelligentsia.

Before the very idea of destroying absolutism by mechanical means could acquire popularity, the state apparatus had to be seen as a purely external organ of coercion, having no roots in the social organization itself. And this is precisely how the Russian autocracy appeared to the revolutionary intelligentsia.

This illusion had its own historical basis. Tsarism took shape under the pressure of the more culturally advanced states of the West. In order to hold its own in competition, it had to bleed the popular masses dry, and in so doing it cut the economic ground from under the feet of even the privileged classes. And these classes were not able to raise themselves to the high political level

---

* A diminutive referring to the two tsars Alexander II and III.

attained by the privileged classes in the West.

To this, in the nineteenth century, was added the powerful pressure of the European stock exchange. The greater the sums it loaned to the tsarist regime, the less tsarism depended directly upon the economic relations within the country.

By means of European capital, it armed itself with European military technology, and it thus grew into a "self-sufficient" (in a relative sense, of course) organization, elevating itself *above all classes of society.*

Such a situation could naturally give rise to the idea of blasting this extraneous superstructure into the air with dynamite.

The intelligentsia felt called upon to carry out this work. Like the state, the intelligentsia had developed under the direct and immediate pressure of the West; like their enemy, the state, they rushed ahead of the country's level of economic development—the state, *technologically;* the intelligentsia, *ideologically.*

Whereas in the older bourgeois societies of Europe revolutionary *ideas* developed more or less parallel with the development of the broad revolutionary *forces,* in Russia the intelligentsia gained access to the ready-made cultural and political ideas of the West and had their thinking revolutionized before the economic development of the country had given birth to serious revolutionary classes from which they could get support.

Under these conditions, nothing remained for the intelligentsia but to multiply their revolutionary enthusiasm by the explosive force of nitroglycerin. So arose the classical terrorism of Narodnaya Volya.

It reached its zenith in two or three years and after that was quickly reduced to nothing, having rapidly consumed in its fiery struggle all the combat reserves that the numerically weak intelligentsia could supply.

The terror of the Social Revolutionaries was by and large a product of those same historical factors: the "self-sufficient" despotism of the Russian state, on the one hand, and the "self-sufficient" Russian revolutionary intelligentsia on the other.

But two decades did not go by without having some effect, and by the time the terrorists of the second wave appear, they do so as *epigones,* marked with the stamp "outdated by history."

The epoch of capitalist "Sturm und Drang" (storm and stress) of the 1880s and 1890s produced and consolidated a large industrial proletariat, making serious inroads into the economic isolation of the countryside and linking it more closely with the factory and the city.

Behind the Narodnaya Volya, there really *was no* revolutionary class. The Social Revolutionaries simply did not *want to see* the revolutionary proletariat; at least they were not able to appreciate its full historical significance.

Of course, one can easily collect a dozen odd quotations from Social Revolutionary literature stating that they pose terror not *instead* of the mass struggle but *together with it.* But these quotations bear witness only to the struggle the ideologists of terror have had to conduct against the Marxists—the theoreticians of mass struggle.

But this does not change matters. Terrorist work, by its very essence, demands such concentrated energy for "the great moment," such an overestimation of the significance of individual heroism, and, finally, such a "hermetic" conspiracy, that—if not logically, then psychologically—it excludes completely any agitational and organizational work among the masses.

For terrorists, in the entire field of politics there exist only two central focuses: the government and the Combat Organization. "The government is ready to temporarily reconcile itself to the existence of all the other currents," Gershuni [a founder of the Combat Organization of the SRs] wrote to his comrades at a time when he was facing the death sentence, "but it has decided to direct all its blows toward crushing the Social Revolutionary Party."

"I sincerely trust," said Kalyaev [another SR terrorist], writing at a similar moment, "that our generation, *headed by the Combat Organization,* will do away with the autocracy."

Everything that is outside the framework of terror is only the setting for the struggle; at best, an auxiliary means. In the blinding flash of exploding bombs, the contours of political parties and the dividing lines of the class struggle disappear without a trace.

And we heard the voice of that greatest of romantics and the best practitioner of the new terrorism, Gershuni, urging his comrades to "avoid a break with not only the ranks of the revolutionaries, but even a break with the opposition parties in general."

"Not *instead* of the masses, but *together with* them." However, terrorism is too "absolute" a form of struggle to be content with a limited and subordinate role in the party.

Engendered by the absence of a revolutionary class, regenerated later by a lack of confidence in the revolutionary masses, terrorism can maintain itself only by exploiting the weakness and disorganization of the masses, minimizing their conquests, and exaggerating their defeats.

"They see that it is impossible, given the nature of modern armaments, for the popular masses to use pitchforks and cudgels—those age-old weapons of the people—to destroy the Bastilles of modern times," defense attorney Zhdanov said of the terrorists during the trial of Kalyaev.

"After January 9* they saw very well what was involved; and they answered the machine gun and rapid-firing rifle with the revolver and the bomb; such are the barricades of the twentieth century."

The revolvers of individual heroes *instead* of the people's cudgels and pitchforks; bombs *instead* of barricades—that is the real formula of terrorism.

And no matter what sort of subordinate role terror is relegated to by the "synthetic" theoreticians of the party, it always occupies a special place of honor in fact. And the Combat Organization, which the official party hierarchy places *under* the Central

---

* A reference to the 'Bloody Sunday' massacre, which marked the start of the 1905 revolution.

Committee, inevitably turns out to be *above* it, *above* the party and all its work—until cruel fate places it *under* the police department.

And that is precisely why the collapse of the Combat Organization as a result of a police conspiracy inevitably means the political collapse of the party as well.

Terrorism and the Stalinist regime in the Soviet Union

In order to justify their use of official terror against the Left Opposition—and virtually the entire old Bolshevik generation—in the bloody purges of the 1930s, Joseph Stalin and his police and judicial apparatus accused them of plotting and engaging in anti-Soviet terrorism, including assassinations and sabotage.

The following testimony by Trotsky was given from exile in Mexico City before members of the International Commission of Inquiry into the Charges Made against Leon Trotsky in the Moscow Trial, on April 17, 1937.

The references to the Kirov assassination refer to Sergei Kirov, leader of the Leningrad Communist Party organization, who was assassinated by Nikolayev in December 1934. Nikolayev had been a supporter of Zinoviev in the 1926–27 United Opposition and his terrorist attack was used as a pretext to bring Zinoviev, Kamenev, and other major leaders of the Russian revolution to trial for inspiring the assassination. (See "The Stalinist Bureaucracy and the Kirov Assassination" in Pathfinder's *Writings of Leon Trotsky (1934–35);* pages 175–97.)

The entire transcript of the hearings of the International Commission of Inquiry, which met from April 10 to April 17, 1937, has been published under the title *The Case of Leon Trotsky* (Pathfinder, 1968). This excerpt appears on pp. 488–94.

If terror is feasible for one side, why should it be considered as excluded for the other? With all its seductive symmetry, this reasoning is corrupt to the core. It is altogether inadmissible to place the terror of a dictatorship against an opposition on the same plane with the terror of an opposition against a dictatorship. To the ruling clique, the preparation of murders through the medium of a court or from behind an ambush is purely and simply a question of police technique. In the event of a failure, some second-rank agents can always be sacrificed. On the part of an opposition, terror presupposes the concentration of all forces upon preparing acts of terror, with the foreknowledge that every one of such acts, whether successful or unsuccessful, will evoke in reply the destruction of scores of its best men. An opposition could by no means permit itself such an insane squandering of its forces. It is precisely for this, and for no other reason, that the Comintern does not resort to terroristic attempts in the countries of fascist dictatorships. The Opposition is as little inclined to the policy of suicide as the Comintern.

According to the indictment, which banks on ignorance and mental laziness, the "Trotskyites" resolved to destroy the ruling group in order in this way to clear for themselves the path to power. The average Philistine, especially if he wears the badge of a "Friend of the U.S.S.R.," reasons as follows: "The Oppositionists could not but strive for power, and could not but hate the ruling group. Why, then, shouldn't they really resort to terror?" In other words, for the Philistine the matter ends where in reality it only begins. The leaders of the Opposition are neither upstarts nor novices. It is not at all a question of whether they were striving for power. Every serious political tendency strives to conquer power. The question is: Could the Oppositionists, educated upon the enormous experience of the revolutionary movement, have entertained even a moment's belief that terror is capable of bringing them closer to power? Russian history, Marxist theory, political psychology reply: No, they could not!

At this point, the problem of terror requires clarification, even though briefly, from the standpoint of history and theory. In so far as I am delineated as the initiator of the "anti-Soviet terror," I am compelled to invest my exposition with an autobiographic character. In 1902 I had no sooner arrived in London from Siberia, after almost five years of prison and exile, than I had the occasion, in a memorial article devoted to the bicentennial of the fortress of Schlusselburg, with its hard-labor prison, to enumerate the revolutionists there tortured to death. "The shades of these martyrs clamor for vengeance. . . ." But immediately thereafter I added: "Not for a personal, but for a revolutionary vengeance. Not for the execution of ministers, but for the execution of the autocracy." These lines were directed wholly against individual terror. Their author was twenty-three years of age. From the earliest days of his revolutionary activity he was already an opponent of terror. From 1902 to 1905 I delivered, in various cities in Europe, before Russian students and emigres, scores of political reports against terrorist ideology, which at the beginning of the century was once again spreading among the Russian youth.

Beginning with the 'eighties of the past century, two generations of Russian Marxists in their personal experience lived through the era of terror, learned from its tragic lessons, and organically instilled in themselves a negative attitude toward the heroic adventurism of lone individuals. Plekhanov, the founder of Russian Marxism; Lenin, the leader of Bolshevism; Martov, the most eminent representative of Menshevism; all dedicated thousands of pages and hundreds of speeches to the struggle against the tactic of terror.

The ideological inspiration emanating from these senior Marxists nourished my attitude toward the revolutionary alchemy of the shut-in intellectual circles during my adolescence. For us, the Russian revolutionists, the problem of terror was a life and death matter in the political as well as the personal meaning of the term.

For us, a terrorist was not a character from a novel, but a living and familiar being. In exile we lived for years side by side with the terrorists of the older generation. In prisons and in police custody we met with terrorists of our own age. We tapped out messages back and forth, in the Peter and Paul fortress, with terrorists condemned to death. How many hours, how many days, were spent in passionate discussion! How many times did we break personal relationships on this most burning of all questions! The Russian literature on terrorism, nourished by and reflecting these debates, would fill a large library.

Isolated terroristic explosions are inevitable whenever political oppression transgresses certain boundaries. Such acts almost always have a symptomatic character. But politics that sanctifies terror, raising it into a system—that is a different thing. "Terrorist work," I wrote in 1909, "by its very essence, demands such concentrated energy for 'the great moment,' such an overestimation of the significance of individual heroism, and finally, such a 'hermetic' conspiracy that . . . it excludes completely any agitational and organizational work among the masses. . . . Struggling against terrorism, the Marxian intelligentsia defended their right or their duty not to withdraw from the working-class districts for the sake of tunneling mines underneath the Grand Ducal and tsarist palaces." It is impossible to fool or outwit history. In the long run, history puts everybody in his place. The basic property of terror as a system is to destroy that organization which by means of chemical compounds seeks to compensate for its own lack of political strength. There are, of course, historical conditions where terror can introduce confusion among the governing ranks. But in that case who is it that can reap the fruits? At all events, not the terrorist organization itself, and not the masses behind whose backs the duel takes place. Thus, the liberal Russian bourgeois, in their day, invariably sympathized with terrorism. The reason is plain. In 1909 I wrote: "In so far as terror introduces disorganization and demoralization into the ranks of the Government (at the price of disorganizing and demoralizing the ranks of the revolutionists), to that extent it plays into the hands of none other than the liberals themselves." The very same idea, expressed virtually in the same words, we meet a quarter of a century later in connection with the Kirov assassination.

The very fact of individual acts of terror is an infallible token of the political backwardness of a country and the feebleness of the progressive forces there. The revolution of 1905, which disclosed the vast strength of the proletariat, put an end to the romanticism of the single combat between a handful of intellectuals and tsarism. "Terrorism in Russia is dead," I reiterated in a number of articles. "Terror has migrated far to the East—to the provinces of Punjab and Bengal. . . . It may be that in other countries of the Orient terrorism is still destined to pass through an epoch of flowering. But in Russia it is already a part of the heritage of history."

In 1907 I found myself again in exile. The whip of counterrevolution was savagely at work, and the Russian colonies in European cities became very numerous. The entire period of my second emigration was devoted to reports and articles against the terror of vengeance and despair. In 1909 it was revealed that at the head of the terrorist organization of the so-called "Social Revolutionists" stood an agent provocateur, Azef. "In the blind alley of terrorism," I wrote, "the hand of provocation rules with assurance" (January, 1910). Terrorism has always remained for me nothing but a "blind alley."

During the same period I wrote: "The irreconcilable attitude of the Russian Social Democracy towards the bureaucratized terror of the revolution as a means of struggle against the terrorist bureaucracy of tsarism has met with bewilderment and condemnation not only among the Russian liberals but also among the European Socialists." Both the latter and the former accused us of "doctrinairism." On our part, we, the Russian Marxists, attributed this sympathy for Russian terrorism to the opportunism of the leaders of European Social Democracy who had become accustomed to transferring their hopes from the masses to the ruling summits. "Whoever stalks a ministerial portfolio . . . as well as those who, clasping an infernal machine beneath a cloak, stalk the Minister himself, must equally *overestimate* the Minister—his personality and his post. For them the *system* itself disappears or recedes far away, and there remains only the *individual* invested with power." We shall presently, in connection with the Kirov assassination, meet once again with this thought, which runs through the decades of my activity.

In 1911 terrorist moods arose among certain groups of Austrian workers. Upon the request of Friedrich Adler, editor of *Der Kampf,* the theoretical monthly of the Austrian Social Democracy, I wrote in November 1911 an article on terrorism for this publication.

Whether a terrorist attempt, even a "successful" one, throws the ruling class into confusion depends on the concrete political circumstances. In any case the confusion can only be short-lived; the capitalist state does not base itself on government ministers and cannot be eliminated with them. The classes it serves will always find new people; the mechanism remains intact and continues to function.

But the disarray introduced into the ranks of the working masses themselves by a terrorist attempt is much deeper. If it is enough to arm oneself with a pistol in order to achieve one's goal, why the efforts of the class struggle? If a thimbleful of gunpowder and a little chunk of lead is enough to shoot the enemy through the neck, what need is there for a class organization? If it makes sense to terrify highly placed personages with the roar of explosions, where is the need for a party? Why meetings, mass agitation, and elections if one can so easily take aim at the ministerial bench from the gallery of parliament?

In our eyes, individual terror is inadmissible precisely because it *belittles the role of the masses in their own conscious-*

ness, reconciles them to their powerlessness, and turns their eyes and hopes toward a great avenger and liberator who some day will come and accomplish his mission.

Five years later, in the heat of the imperialist war, Friedrich Adler, who had spurred me to write this article, killed the Austrian minister-president Stuergkh in a Vienna restaurant. The heroic skeptic and opportunist was unable to find any other outlet for his indignation and despair. My sympathies were, naturally, not on the side of the Hapsburg dignitary. However, to the individualist action of Friedrich Adler, I counterposed the form of activity of Karl Liebknecht who, during wartime, went out into a Berlin square to distribute a revolutionary manifesto to the workers.

On the 28th of December, 1934, four weeks after the Kirov assassination, at a time when the Stalinist judiciary did not know as yet in which direction to aim the barb of their "justice," I wrote in the *Bulletin of the Opposition:*

> . . . If Marxists have categorically condemned individual terrorism . . . even when the shots were directed against the agents of the tsarist government and of capitalist exploitation, then all the more relentlessly will they condemn and reject the criminal adventurism of terrorist acts directed against the bureaucratic representatives of the first workers state in history. The subjective motivations of Nikolayev and his associates are a matter of indifference to us. The road to hell is paved with good intentions. So long as the Soviet bureaucracy has not been removed by the proletariat—a task which will eventually be accomplished—it fulfills a necessary function in the defense of the workers state. Should terrorism of the Nikolayev type spread, it could, given other unfavorable circumstances, render service only to the fascist counterrevolution.
>
> Only political fakers who bank on imbeciles would en-

deavor to lay Nikolayev at the door of the Left Opposition, even if only in the guise of the Zinoviev group as it existed in 1926–27. The terrorist organization of the Communist youth is fostered not by the Left Opposition but by the bureaucracy, by its internal decomposition. *Individual terrorism in its very essence is bureaucratism turned inside out.* For Marxists this law was not discovered yesterday. Bureaucratism has no confidence in the masses, and endeavors to substitute itself for the masses. Terrorism behaves in the same manner; it wants to make the masses happy without asking their participation. The Stalinist bureaucracy has created a revolting leader-cult, endowing leaders with divine attributes. The 'hero' cult is also the religion of terrorism, only with a minus sign. The Nikolayevs imagine that all that is necessary is to remove a few leaders by means of revolvers, in order for history to take another course. Communist-terrorists, as an ideological grouping, are of the same flesh and blood as the Stalinist bureaucracy. [January, 1935, No. 41.] [The entire article is reprinted in *Writings of Leon Trotsky (1934–35)* (Pathfinder, 1971) pp. 175–97.]

These lines, as you have had the opportunity to convince yourselves, were not written *ad hoc.* They summarize the experience of a whole lifetime, which was in turn fed by the experience of two generations.

Already in the epoch of tsarism, a young Marxist who went over to the ranks of the terrorist party was a comparatively rare phenomenon—rare enough to cause people to point their fingers. But at that time there was at least taking place an unceasing theoretical struggle between two tendencies; the publications of the two parties were waging a bitter polemic; public disputes did not cease for a single day. Now, on the other hand, they want to force us to believe that not young revolutionists, but old leaders of Russian Marxism, with the tradition of three revolutions behind them, have suddenly, without criticism, without discussion, without a single word of explanation, turned their faces toward the terrorism which they had always rejected as a method of political suicide. The very possibility of such an accusation shows to what depths of debasement the Stalinist bureaucracy has dragged the official theoretical and political thought, not to mention Soviet justice. To political convictions gained through experience, sealed by theory, tempered in the white heat of the history of mankind, the falsifiers counterpose inchoate, contradictory, and utterly unsubstantiated testimonies of suspicious nonentities.

For Grynszpan: Against the fascist pogrom gangs and Stalinist scoundrels

Herschel Grynszpan assassinated a Nazi official in the German embassy in Paris on November 7, 1938. Trotsky's article on the assassination first appeared in the February 14, 1939, *Socialist Appeal*. It is reprinted here from *Writings of Leon Trotsky (1938–39)*, published by Pathfinder.

It is clear to anyone even slightly acquainted with political history that the policy of the fascist gangsters directly and sometimes deliberately provokes terrorist acts. What is most astonishing is that so far there has been only one Grynszpan. Undoubtedly the number of such acts will increase.

We Marxists consider the tactic of individual terror inexpedient in the tasks of the liberating struggle of the proletariat as well as oppressed nationalities. A single isolated hero cannot replace the masses. But we understand only too clearly the inevitability of such convulsive acts of despair and vengeance. All our emotions, all our sympathies are with the self-sacrificing avengers even though they have been unable to discover the correct road.

Our sympathy becomes intensified because Grynszpan is not a political militant but an inexperienced youth, almost a boy, whose only counselor was a feeling of indignation. To tear Grynszpan out of the hands of capitalist justice, which is capable of chopping off his head to further serve capitalist diplomacy, is the elementary, immediate task of the international working class!

All the more revolting in its police stupidity and inexpressible violence is the campaign now being conducted against Grynszpan by command of the Kremlin in the international Stalinist press. They attempt to depict him as an agent of the Nazis or an agent of Trotskyists in alliance with the Nazis. Lumping into one heap the provocateur and his victim, the Stalinists ascribe to Grynszpan the intention of creating a favorable pretext for Hitler's pogrom measures. What can one say of these venal "journalists" who no longer have any vestiges of shame? Since the beginning of the socialist movement the bourgeoisie has at all times attributed all violent demonstrations of indignation, particularly terrorist acts, to the degenerating influence of Marxism. The Stalinists have inherited, here as elsewhere, the filthiest tradition of reaction. The Fourth International may, justifiably, be proud that the reactionary scum, including the Stalinists, now automatically links with the Fourth International every bold action and protest, every indignant outburst, every blow at the executioners.

It was so, similarly, with the International of Marx in its time. We are bound, naturally, by ties of open moral solidarity to Grynszpan and not to his "democratic" jailers, or the Stalinist slanderers who need Grynszpan's corpse to prop up, even if only partially and indirectly, the verdicts of Moscow justice. Kremlin diplomacy, degenerated to its marrow, attempts at the same time to utilize this "Happy" incident to renew their machinations for an international agreement among various governments, including that of Hitler and Mussolini, for a mutual extradition of terrorists. Beware, masters of fraud! The application of such a law will necessitate the immediate deliverance of Stalin to at least a dozen foreign governments.

The Stalinists shriek in the ears of the police that Grynszpan attended "meetings of Trotskyites." That, unfortunately, is not true. For had he walked into the milieu of the Fourth International he would have discovered a different and more effective outlet for his revolutionary energy. People come cheap who are capable only of fulminating against injustice and bestiality. But those who, like Grynszpan, are able to act as well as conceive, sacrificing their own lives if need be, are the precious leaven of mankind.

In the moral sense, although not for his mode of action, Grynszpan may serve as an example for every young revolutionist. Our open moral solidarity with Grynszpan gives us an added right to say to all the other would-be Grynszpans, to all those capable of self-sacrifice in the struggle against despotism and bestiality: *Seek another road!* Not the lone avenger but only a great revolutionary mass movement can free the oppressed, a movement that will leave no remnant of the entire structure of class exploitation, national oppression, and racial persecution. The unprecedented crimes of fascism create a yearning for vengeance that is wholly justifiable. But so monstrous is the scope of their crimes, that this yearning cannot be satisfied by the assassination of isolated fascist bureaucrats. For that it is necessary to set in motion millions, tens and hundreds of millions of the oppressed throughout the whole world and lead them in the assault upon the strongholds of the old society. Only the overthrow of all forms of slavery, only the complete destruction of fascism, only the people sitting in merciless judgment over the contemporary bandits and gangsters can provide real satisfaction to the indignation of the people. This is precisely the task that the Fourth International has set itself. It will cleanse the labor movement of the plague of Stalinism. It will rally in its ranks the heroic generation of the youth. It will cut a path to a worthier and a more humane future.

Also from Pathfinder

CAPITALISM'S WORLD DISORDER

Jack Barnes

The social devastation and financial panic, the coarsening of politics, the cop brutality and acts of imperialist aggression accelerating around us—all are the product not of something gone wrong but of the lawful workings of capitalism. Yet the future can be changed by the united struggle and selfless action of workers and farmers conscious of their power to transform the world. $24. Also in Spanish and French.

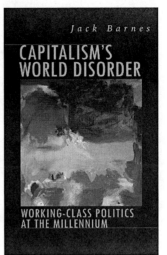

THE COMMUNIST MANIFESTO

Karl Marx and Frederick Engels

Founding document of the modern working-class movement, published in 1848. Explains why communism is not a set of preconceived principles but the line of march of the working class toward power, "springing from an existing class struggle, a historical movement going on under our very eyes." $5. Also in Spanish.

TEAMSTER REBELLION

Farrell Dobbs

The 1934 strikes that built the industrial union movement in Minneapolis and helped pave the way for the CIO, recounted by a central leader of that battle. The first in a four-volume series on the class-struggle leadership of the strikes and organizing drives that transformed the Teamsters union in much of the Midwest into a fighting social movement and pointed the road toward independent labor political action. $19. Also in Spanish.

THE CHANGING FACE OF U.S. POLITICS
WORKING-CLASS POLITICS AND THE TRADE UNIONS
Jack Barnes

Building the kind of party working people need to prepare for coming class battles through which they will organize and strengthen the unions, as they revolutionize themselves and all society. A handbook for those repelled by the class inequalities, racism, women's oppression, cop violence, and wars inherent in capitalism, for those who are seeking the road toward effective action to overturn that exploitative system and join in reconstructing the world on new, socialist foundations. $24. Also in Spanish and French.

THE HISTORY OF THE RUSSIAN REVOLUTION
Leon Trotsky

The social, economic, and political dynamics of the first socialist revolution as told by one of its central leaders. "The history of a revolution is for us first of all a history of the forcible entrance of the masses into the realm of rulership over their own destiny," Trotsky writes. Unabridged edition, 3 vols. in one. $36. Also in Russian.

THE STRUGGLE FOR A PROLETARIAN PARTY
James P. Cannon

"The workers of America have power enough to topple the structure of capitalism at home and to lift the whole world with them when they rise," Cannon asserts. On the eve of World War II, a founder of the communist movement in the United States and leader of the Communist International in Lenin's time defends the program and party-building norms of Bolshevism. $22. Also in Spanish.

THE WORKING CLASS AND THE TRANSFORMATION OF LEARNING

THE FRAUD OF EDUCATION REFORM
UNDER CAPITALISM

Jack Barnes

"Until society is reorganized so that education is a human activity from the time we are very young until the time we die, there will be no education worthy of working, creating humanity." $3. Also in Spanish, French, Icelandic, Swedish, Farsi, and Greek.

IMPERIALISM, THE HIGHEST STAGE OF CAPITALISM

V.I. Lenin

"I trust that this pamphlet will help the reader to understand the fundamental economic question, that of the economic essence of imperialism," Lenin wrote in 1917. "For unless this is studied, it will be impossible to understand and appraise modern war and modern politics." $10. Also in Spanish.

TO SPEAK THE TRUTH

WHY WASHINGTON'S 'COLD WAR'
AGAINST CUBA DOESN'T END

Fidel Castro, Ernesto Che Guevara

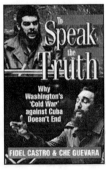

In historic speeches before the United Nations General Assembly and other UN bodies, Guevara and Castro address the peoples of the world, explaining why the U.S. government fears the example of the socialist revolution in Cuba and why Washington's effort to destroy it will fail. $17

OUR HISTORY IS STILL BEING WRITTEN

THE STORY OF THREE CHINESE-CUBAN GENERALS
IN THE CUBAN REVOLUTION

Armando Choy, Gustavo Chui, and Moisés Sío Wong talk about the historic place of Chinese immigration to Cuba, as well as more than five decades of revolutionary action and internationalism, from Cuba to Angola and Venezuela today. Through their stories we see the social and political forces that gave birth to the Cuban nation and opened the door to the socialist revolution in the Americas. We see how millions of ordinary men and women changed the course of history, becoming different human beings in the process. $20. Also in Spanish, Chinese.

New International
A MAGAZINE OF MARXIST POLITICS AND THEORY

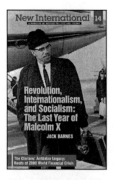

New International no. 14

Revolution, Internationalism, and Socialism: The Last Year of Malcolm X *by Jack Barnes* • The Clintons' Antilabor Legacy: Roots of the 2008 Financial Crisis *by Jack Barnes* • The Stewardship of Nature Also Falls to the Working Class: In Defense of Land and Labor *Socialist Workers Party resolution* $14

New International no. 13

Our Politics Start with the World *by Jack Barnes* • Farming, Science, and the Working Classes *by Steve Clark* • Capitalism, Labor, and Nature: An Exchange *Richard Levins, Steve Clark* $14

New International no. 12

Their Transformation and Ours *Socialist Workers Party 2005 world political resolution* • Capitalism's Long Hot Winter Has Begun *by Jack Barnes* • Crisis, Boom, and Revolution *1921 reports by V.I. Lenin and Leon Trotsky* $16

New International no. 10

Imperialism's March toward Fascism and War *by Jack Barnes* • What the 1987 Stock Market Crash Foretold • Defending Cuba, Defending Cuba's Socialist Revolution *by Mary-Alice Waters* $16

Order from www.pathfinderpress.com
Most of these articles are also available in Spanish in *Nueva Internacional*, and in French in *Nouvelle Internationale*.
Some are also available in Swedish in *Ny International*.